THE GREEN CROSS OF KAFIRA

FRANCIS D. IMBUGA

Foreword by
Prof. Kurtz Rogers

BOOKMARK AFRICA
Pushing boundaries

Bookmark Africa Publishers
P.O. Box 14915-00800 Westlands, Nairobi, Kenya

First published 2013

© 2013 Francis Imbuga
ISBN   978-9966-05-539-2
ebook edition available ISBN   978-9966-05-540-8

KNLS Cataloguing in Publication data
Imbuga, Francis
    The green cross of Kafira / by Francis Imbuga. –
Nairobi: Bookmark Africa, 2013.
        p.   cm.
        e -ISBN   978-9966-05-540-8
        ISBN   978-9966-05-539-2 (printed version)

        1. Literature. 2. African Literature (English) – plays.
        3. African authors - Imbuga, Francis – Political. 4. Dictatorship of the
        proletariat. I. Title.

828.99676202 -- dc 22

PR9381.9.I4 G74 2013

Book and cover design by Tony Okuku

CONTENTS

FOREWORD

Before his untimely death in November 2012, Prof. Francis D. Imbuga was among the most productive and respected of Kenya's contemporary writers and scholars. In a remembrance published in the *East African* magazine, Anne Manyara highlights Imbuga's significant role in Kenyan literary history, suggesting that he will be recalled as "an icon – a prolific writer, an astute playwright, an excellent actor." This assessment is typical of the numerous accolades that poured forth on the occasion of Prof. Imbuga's passing.

Born in 1947 – a decade after literary pioneers such as Grace Ogot, Ngugi wa Thiong'o, Okot p'Bitek and Taban lo Liyong – Imbuga was a leading member of what might be termed a "second generation" of East African writers. He came of age at a time when East African literature was forging a tentative early identity, and he participated in the exciting and innovative process of developing and extending that identity. Although he is most widely known for his work as a playwright and actor, Imbuga's prodigious creative energies also encompassed other genres such as poetry, narrative, television and film, in addition to his work as a teacher, scholar, and university administrator.

His rural upbringing in Western Kenya and the strong oral traditions characterizing that upbringing have informed both the themes and the style of Imbuga's works, which were also impacted by formal study at the highest levels. His early academic achievements earned him a place at the elite Alliance High School (Nairobi), where he pursued his secondary school studies from 1964 to 1969, and where he began to deliberately explore his interest in drama. As a student at the University of Nairobi in the early 1970s, in addition to his regular studies he continued his acting career, publishing three plays and composing many others, along with writing, directing and acting in over fifty dramatic productions for the Voice of Kenya television's African Theatre Series. During this time, the renowned Ghanaian playwright, Joe de Graft, then teaching at the University of Nairobi on a UNESCO grant, was commissioned to write the play *Muntu*. This production, featuring an all-star cast with a memorable performance by Imbuga in one of the leading roles, is remembered as a landmark in Kenyan theatre performance, and helped solidify Imbuga's reputation as a leading figure in Kenyan drama.

After graduating from the University of Nairobi, where he earned both bachelor's and master's degrees, Imbuga continued to balance his academic vocation with a highly productive writing career. He studied at University College in Cardiff (Wales) from 1974 to 1975, was involved in theatre workshops and productions in Ghana in the mid-1970s, and participated in UNESCO – sponsored workshops in Zaire (1979), Paris (1980) and Sofia (1982). He completed a PhD in English at the University of Iowa and also participated in that university's acclaimed International Writing Programme from 1988 to 1991. In 1994-95, he was a Fulbright Scholar-in-Residence at Tennessee State University. Beginning in 1999, he spent several years in Rwanda as a dean at the Kigali Institute of Education. In between these posts, he served as a professor and administrator at Kenyatta University.

Despite his wide travel and international studies, Imbuga's professional and creative work has always focused on Kenya, and his writing has inevitably contained frank discussion and criticism of the region's contemporary social issues. There runs through all of Imbuga's work a notable theme of social criticism, a concern with issues of cultural identity, and above all a powerful, sympathetic sense of humour in the face of the vagaries and ironies of life. Several of his plays foreground the megalomaniacal tendencies of political leaders. An early play, *The Married Bachelor* (1973) was revised to include more development of its female characters under the title of *The Burning of Rags* (1989). *Aminata* was written in support of the goals of the United Nations Decade for Women. *The Return of Mgofu* (2011) spotlights genocide and ethnic conflict. The novel *The Miracle of Remera* (2004) represents a commentary on East Africa's AIDS crisis, while Imbuga's best novel, *Shrine of Tears* (1993), is a *roman à clef* dealing with the personalities and events connected with the Kenya National Theatre during the 1970s and 1980s.

In the first full-length scholarly study of Imbuga's works, the Ugandan playwright John Ruganda describes Imbuga as a master of "transparent concealment" – someone who found a way to write socially critical drama in a charged political atmosphere that was essentially antagonistic towards writers in general and theatre in particular. The title of Ruganda's study is apt; Imbuga, claims Ruganda, found a way of "Telling the Truth Laughingly".

The Green Cross of Kafira was intended as a late-arriving conclusion to a trilogy of plays set in the fictional nation of Kafira. While they may readily be appreciated independently, the three plays as a collection offer an excellent overview of Imbuga's style of pointed "truth-telling" about contemporary African politics and society. They are more overtly political than some of his other plays, which focus on interpersonal or family dramas. Put together, the "Kafira Trilogy" highlights the betrayal of trust on both personal and political levels in postcolonial Africa, indicting corruption and greed while still maintaining an optimistic hope for social change.

The first Kafira play remains his most popular; *Betrayal in the City* was first performed at the Kenya National Theatre in 1975, and published by Heinemann Kenya the following year. In 1977 the play was selected as one of Kenya's official entries to the Second World Black and African Festival of Arts and Culture (FESTAC) in Lagos, and it was recently named (for the third time) as a set text for Kenyan secondary school students. *Betrayal* explores the political psychology of African dictatorship, featuring varied responses to the repressive rule of a head of state named "Boss." Truth-telling in such a setting becomes tricky and dangerous, a reality highlighted by the principled but unstable character of Jusper, who writes plays that cannot be published because in them the *"truth is too much in the nude."*

Man of Kafira, the second title in the Kafira Trilogy, was first performed in 1979 and published five years later. Some of the characters from *Betrayal* reappear, but under changed circumstances. "Boss" has been deposed as leader of Kafira and is living in exile in the nation of Abiara. Complex intrigues involve religious leaders, Boss's wives, his exilic host Gafi, the new Kafiran president, and the returned Jusper. In *Man of Kafira*, we see again the themes of political and personal betrayal, with questions about the role of art in such a setting brought even more to the fore.

Because it was written decades after the earlier Kafira plays, the emphasis in *The Green Cross of Kafira* is more contemporary than the first parts of the trilogy. The play criticizes the land-grabbing practices of the political elite that result in ecological disaster, which the play presents as being at once a spiritual and a material problem. Imbuga dedicated the play to the memory of the late Wangari Mathaai, who received the 2004 Nobel Peace Prize for her longstanding environmental activism that at times brought strong retaliation from entrenched business and political interests. The work is ultimately optimistic: *"To tell you the truth,"* concludes the narrator Sikia Macho, *"I can't wait for tomorrow."* Readers and admirers of Imbuga's work will unfortunately experience that tomorrow without him, but we can be consoled in part by the wealth of creative works that he left behind.

Dr. J. Roger Kurtz
State University of New York
(Brockport)

The Green Cross of Kafira

Dedicated to Wangari Maathai
who was born on April Fools' Day,
but saw the need to
conserve, nurture and protect the natural.

List of Characters

Kafira is an imaginary African state in its fourth decade of self-rule.

Sikia Macho:	The narrator of the story of The Green Cross of Kafira
Mwodi:	An official in the Government of Kafira
Yuda:	An official in the Government of Kafira
Bishop Ben'sa:	Head of The Green Cross of Kafira
Sister Leah:	Bishop Ben'sa's personal assistant
Pastor Mgei:	Founder of The Green Cross Clinic, now a detainee
George Adema:	A final year Masters student, now a detainee
Mama Mgei:	Wife of Pastor Mgei, now in charge of the Green Cross Clinic
Reject One:	Ex-policeman, now perceived as a dissident
Reject Two:	Ex-trade unionist, now perceived as a dissident
Reject Three:	Ex-student leader, now perceived as a dissident
Reject Four:	A conservationist, now perceived as a female dissident
Reject Five:	Ex-Rector at the Kafira University of Natural Wisdom, now perceived as a dissident
Choreographer:	Hired to train the rejects.
Two school children	
Serikali:	Swahili word for government.

ACT ONE: SCENE ONE

Mind Games

A conversation of traditional instruments can be heard from a distance. A male voice sings above the instruments. He is obviously enjoying himself. The singer's voice becomes stronger as he gets closer. His name is Sikia Macho.

Sikia Macho: *(Enters still singing. He dances briefly, stops and surveys the audience critically.)* Aah, the coast is clear. For awhile, just for one short while, I thought it was a case of the proverbial walls that have ears. *(Pause)* My name is Sikia Macho, which means listen to your eyes or hear your eyes. But to those who are endowed with the ability for deep thought, it simply means the observer. I am a great grandson of the Sikia Macho who begot the Sikia Macho who begot the Sikia Macho who begot me. For your information, all those Sikia Machos before me were great orators. They were great storytellers too. You will be glad to know that I am no exception. I am here to share with you the political history of the Republic of Kafira. So, you better prepare to listen with both ears. *(Interlude of musical instruments fills the air.)* The Republic of Kafira attained her self-rule more than three decades ago. During all this time, Kafira has been ruled by a rich variety of leaders; some good, others not so good while the rest were outright disasters. My story today is the story of the experiences of people of Kafira during the rule of one of the most nervous regimes our country has ever had. So welcome to the games of rhetoric and silence that characterised the rule of that particular regime, the regime of the Chief of Chiefs. *(Sikia Macho exits as curtains open to the sound of traffic on a busy road. A car slows down and stops by the roadside. After hooting, a second car, going in the same direction, stops behind the first one. A man, Mwodi, gets out of the second car and walks towards the first car. Another man, Yuda, gets out of the first car and the two greet each other enthusiastically.)*

Mwodi:	Good evening Honourable Yuda.
Yuda:	Good evening my brother.
Mwodi:	Do you want to die before you defend your seat?
Yuda:	Why?
Mwodi:	You were driving too fast.
Yuda:	It's this double security thing from the Chief of Chiefs. No personal drivers,

no reporters and no bodyguards. Period. Orders from above.

Mwodi: That made me nervous too. All of a sudden it is as if all our lives are in great danger. In fact this whole thing is very contradictory. I mean, if this mission is as important as it is dangerous, the more reason for the services of our personal drivers and bodyguards.

Yuda: No, on second thought, I think you are mistaken there. The mission may be highly sensitive, but I wouldn't classify it as dangerous; it is only a top-secret mission.

Mwodi: Top-secret mission?

Yuda: Yes, a highly sensitive matter given its timing so close to the ballot.

Mwodi: Since when did the need for reconciliation become top-secret?

Yuda: The Chief of Chiefs calls it a reconciliation mission but you and I know that he doesn't mean it. This is a case of surprise and attack. Don't forget that. It is the element of surprise that will win back the people's support. That is not an ordinary market-place strategy you know. The Chief of Chiefs is a good strategist I tell you. Let's give credit where it is due.

Mwodi: That may be a good strategy, but I think it is a case of too little too late.

Yuda:	Too little too late? You are wrong. It is never too late where the element of surprise is applied.
Mwodi:	But what about the opinion polls?
Yuda:	What opinion polls? Polls before the actual polls? Forget them. After all they are conducted by people who know nothing about how we do things here. My brother in politics, experience will carry the day, not opinion polls. So, don't worry.
Mwodi:	It's their consistency that worries me.
Yuda:	Look, we know who is behind the manipulation of those opinion polls, and we will soon prove them all wrong.
Mwodi:	Alright, for now you win; but let us agree on one thing before we proceed.
Yuda:	What?
Mwodi:	When we get there, you'll do most of the talking.
Yuda:	Hon. Mwodi, when the Chief of Chiefs appointed us for this mission, he didn't give us guidelines on how much each one of us should talk.
Mwodi:	It's a favour. I am asking for a favour.
Yuda:	A favour? What favour?
Mwodi:	You know I don't know how to talk to Christians. I mean to religious people. I just don't know how to talk to them. And

	she is a woman too. I don't know how to talk to a woman bishop.
Yuda:	Hon. Mwodi we've done our research, Bishop Ben'sa is a very down-to-earth woman. She may be tough, intimidating and all that, but she's sensible and very reasonable. She's respectful too and I can assure you that she'll talk to us the way people should talk to one another.
Mwodi:	You know it is said that she has super-natural powers. I mean, is she not the one who predicted those ethnic clashes at Koru? They say she can read people's minds.
Yuda:	So what if she can?
Mwodi:	I hate being on the defensive. What if she brings up that taboo subject?
Yuda:	What taboo subject?
Mwodi:	She might bring up the matter of release of that fake pastor.
Yuda:	Which pastor?
Mwodi:	How many pastors do we have in detention?
Yuda:	I am sure she will not bring it up.
Mwodi:	But between you and me...
Yuda:	Bishop Ben'sa is not as naive as you think. The matter of Pastor Mgei's detention is a taboo subject that should be avoided like the plague and she knows it.

Mwodi:	But we need to be prepared for any eventuality.
Yuda:	If she brings up the matter we can always turn to strategy number two.
Mwodi:	Strategy number two? Do we have a second strategy?
Yuda:	But of course we do. Brother Mwodi, I think you were too young when they thrust you into this game of politics. If she brings up the subject of the release of that troublemaker, leave it to me. In fact, that would prove that that is their single most important preoccupation, and that is when we would turn to our next strategy.
Mwodi:	Why do I have to struggle to get such vital information from you?
Yuda:	No harm intended. Remember state secrets are not bananas for sale. You must learn to bite off what you can chew. Don't forget that.
Mwodi:	I will remember it if you tell me what this second strategy is all about.
Yuda:	We can link the Pastor Mgei demonstrations to her NGO and threaten to deregister it. Alternatively, we could just postpone the elections and spread rumours of the imminent release of Pastor Mgei and see what happens.
Mwodi:	Diversion of the national mind?

Yuda:	Absolutely. It is dangerous to let a nation think about one thing for too long. (*Looks at his watch*) Oh, come, we are getting late. We should be on our way. We will talk about strategies later.
Mwodi:	Will you be taping?
Yuda:	Why do you ask?
Mwodi:	Curiosity.
Yuda:	(*Pointing to his belt*) My belt will. (*They go back to their respective vehicles and drive off.*)

SCENE TWO

Seeds of Discord

(The scene is a sitting room at the residence of Bishop Ben'sa at the Headquarters of The Green Cross of Kafira. The room is furnished to reflect the religious beliefs which members of the organisation stand for. Bishop Ben'sa, appropriately adorned, sits on a chair. Opposite her sits Sister Leah. The two are rehearsing a new song.)

Ben'sa: *(Singing in a low tone)*

Welcome to The Green Cross

Where all members are free

Welcome to The Green Cross

Cradle of our future

Welcome to The Green Cross

We sing and pray together.

Ben'sa: I think we should change the lyrics a little.

Instead of, *"Cradle of our future"* why don't we simply say, *"Cradle of our times"*? What do you think?

Sister Leah: I think so too. "Cradle of our future" sounds a bit flat, I mean what about now? The cradle is here with us, isn't it?

Ben'sa: Cradle of our times, it is. Let's try it.

(Both sing) Welcome to The Green Cross

Where all members are free
Welcome to The Green Cross
Cradle of our times
Welcome to The Green Cross
Where all members are free
Welcome to The Green Cross
We sing and pray together.

Ben'sa: That is much better. *(A doorbell rings and Leah goes to answer it.)*

Leah: Hello. Okay, I will be right there. *(To Ben'sa)* The visitors have arrived.

Ben'sa: See them in. *(Leah exits. Outside we hear the opening and closing of car doors. Footsteps approach, then a knock at the door.)*

Ben'sa: *(Standing up)* Yes, come right in. *(Sister Leah ushers the visitors in.)*

Ben'sa: Welcome, gentlemen.

Mwodi & Yuda: Thank you Bishop. *(Ben'sa shakes their hands.)*

Ben'sa: Sister Leah, please say a short prayer to thank our Maker and welcome the visitors.

Sister Leah: Let us pray. *(During the short prayer all but Yuda close their eyes.)* Almighty God, you who rules the sky and the earth, we thank you for this day and for the days gone. We thank you, our Father, for the safety of our visitors as they travelled

9

to honour their commitment. Lord, with humility, we ask that you grant us the wisdom to consult with honesty and dignity. Father, relax our minds, so that we may talk to one another as people to people. I ask this through the name of your son, Jesus Christ.

All: Amen.

Ben'sa: Please take seats and feel at home. Well, well, well, I don't remember when we were last honoured with a visit by officials from *Serikali*. Hon. Mwodi, sorry for what happened to you two weeks ago. I hope you are now feeling much better.

Mwodi: Yes, Bishop, I am feeling fine. Thank God it was only a minor accident.

Ben'sa: We praise the Lord for that. *(Clears her throat)* Gentlemen, Sister Leah here is my personal assistant. *(Both bow)* I have asked her to record our deliberations.

Yuda: Well, Bishop, because of the nature of our consultations today, we did not feel it necessary to bring our personal assistants with us.

Ben'sa: I see. But are you sure you won't want anything put down?

Mwodi: No, Bishop, that will not be necessary. We intend this to be a kind of brainstorming session.

Ben'sa: Very well then, Sister Leah you may take your leave. *(Sister Leah exits)* Gentlemen, you may proceed.

Yuda: Bishop as you probably know, *Serikali* is getting very concerned about a few evil-minded individuals in our midst. These individuals, it seems, are determined to paint your organisation and the state as sworn enemies. You have probably noticed this in the local media. The Chief of Chiefs is particularly disturbed about this turn of events. He wants the organisation, and particularly your Church, The Green Cross Church, to work hand in hand with *Serikali* in order to develop this God-given land of ours. That is why he sent us here.

Mwodi: That is why he takes every opportunity to encourage us leaders in *Serikali* to listen to what church leaders say and do and to support them.

Yuda: That is true. Take me, for example, since the beginning of the year there is no single Sunday I have missed going to church.

Mwodi: Me too, until I got involved in that accident.

Ben'sa: That is all very commendable gentlemen. Only remember that he who brags of being an early riser deserves to be asked

	what he does once he wakes up. *(Mwodi and Yuda are visibly embarrassed.)* Yes, it is not how early you wake up, but what you do after waking up. That is what matters.
Mwodi:	True, true, but if it is the matter of paying tithes and...
Ben'sa:	That is not what I meant Hon. Mwodi. You know you can be a perfectly honourable Christian without paying tithes. But that aside, I still don't understand how our organisation can assist you in this matter of *Serikali* and the media.
Yuda:	Bishop, let me put it this way: it is sometimes good to call a spade a spade and I believe...
Ben'sa:	It is always good to call a spade a spade because that is what it is. Remember, truth is heavenly.
Yuda:	I agree.
Mwodi:	Me too, truth is heavenly.
Yuda:	Bishop, as you are no doubt aware, in the matter of the abduction of the two visiting priests from your Church *Serikali* had no hand in it. That is why we will leave no...
Ben'sa:	...stone unturned until the culprits are brought to book.
Yuda:	Absolutely. So why does the media think that somehow *Serikali* had something to do with it? Where is the evidence?

Ben'sa: The disappearance of our priests after their abduction should be the concern of every self-respecting Kafiran. Those two were here to assist us in our struggle for the improvement of the human condition in Kafira. They were here to assist us in the fight against poverty and ignorance. What wrong did they do that they should vanish into thin air under mysterious circumstances? As a church, our immediate concern is the now familiar harassment of known members of our movement by agents of *Serikali*.

Yuda: Bishop, the people behind those acts are in fact criminals out to tarnish the good name of *Serikali*. In fact, we now have concrete evidence that some of them are actually residing at The Green Cross Clinic.

Ben'sa: Really?

Yuda: Yes.

Ben'sa: Hon. Yuda, as far as we the Church are concerned, The Green Cross Clinic is a hospital where the insecure in mind go for natural healing. It is not a den of criminals. The fact that the name of the clinic is Green Cross does not necessarily mean that the patients who attend the clinic are members of The Green Cross of Kafira, neither does it mean that they are members of The Green Cross Church.

Mwodi:	But Bishop, in all honesty, you must agree with us that the activities at that so-called clinic are not devoid of politics.
Ben'sa:	There is politics and there is politics. There is the hard politics of power and government and there is the politics of general human existence.
Yuda:	But gathering at the clinic to incite people is not...
Ben'sa:	Aren't you forgetting something? Although Pastor Mgei is now retired, the people still see him as the symbol of their well-being. His detention without trial only added insult to injury. Those who gather there go there to empathise with the pastor's family. It is as simple as that. But if you think that those who go there, go there to engage in political activities, then the logical thing would be to go there, arrest and take them to court.
Yuda:	No, Bishop, that is easier said than done. This is an election year and we do not want our people to harm one another as they did four years ago. That is why we have come to you. We need your advice because we want to promote peaceful co-existence.
Ben'sa:	Be truthful and tell me why you have come. By going round in circles you are in fact inviting me to join you in wasting *Serikali's* valuable time.

Mwodi:	We need your advice.
Ben'sa:	In what?
Yuda:	Let me call a spade a spade.
Ben'sa:	Yes, Hon. Yuda, you had better, it is about time. I don't remember the last time that anyone in *Serikali* ever called a spade a spade.
Yuda:	Bishop, let me jog your mind. You will remember that at the time of Pastor Mgei's arrest for incitement, he had not fully paid the land rates for the plot in which Green Cross Clinic now stands.
Ben'sa:	Yes, I remember.
Yuda:	At that time, *Serikali* wanted to reclaim it and turn it into a modern City Park, do you remember?
Ben'sa:	Yes, as well as I remember yesterday.
Yuda:	And when you personally went to the Chief of Chiefs to request him to give the family time to pay the balance, what did he do? Do you remember?
Ben'sa:	Of course I remember that. How can I forget the kindness of the Chief of Chiefs? Why, I even remember the very words he used as he gave me and the Mgei family a grace period of two weeks. How can I forget that?
Yuda:	Would he have done that if he was a stone-hearted man?

Ben'sa:	The naked truth is that the Chief of Chiefs did not believe we could raise the balance of the land rates arrears in two weeks.
Yuda:	How can you say that? Where is the evidence?
Ben'sa:	The Chief of Chiefs looked straight at me and said, "Bishop, *Serikali* regrets the abduction of two of your priests and I can assure you that no stone shall be left unturned until those responsible are brought to book. However, in the matter of the pastor's land deals, *Serikali* cannot interfere with the business of the court. *(Long pause)* But on second thought, being a fair man, I will try to persuade the court to give the family two more weeks within which the balance of payment for The Green Cross plot must be paid fully or the land will be reclaimed for development." Those were his very words.
Yuda:	You have a good head.
Ben'sa:	I thank my creator for it.
Mwodi:	Just out of curiosity, you took everyone by surprise when you raised the arrears in exactly ten days. Where did you get the money from?
Ben'sa:	Well-wishers.
Mwodi:	Well-wishers? Were they sponsors or well-wishers?

Ben'sa:	What is in a name? We call those who assisted us well-wishers, but you prefer to call them sponsors. We do not wish to object to your choice of name for them.
Yuda:	Now you remember I said I wanted to call a spade a spade?
Ben'sa:	Yes, I have a good head, I remember that.
Yuda:	Are those well-wishers the same ones trying to sponsor Mama Mgei to stand against the Chief of Chiefs in the forth-coming general election?
Ben'sa:	My name is Bishop Ben'sa; I am not Counsellor Mama Mgei. We stick to the business of our calling as you have repeatedly told us. But Mama Mgei is not a bishop, neither is she a pastor of a Church. Her allegiance is only to her conscience.
Yuda:	But are you aware that members of your organisation are planning to launch a new political party?
Ben'sa:	No. Ours is a Church, hers a clinic.
Yuda:	Bishop Ben'sa, since Counsellor Mama Mgei is a member of your Church, we have come to plead with you to persuade her not to be misled into forming a political party at the moment. That would create unnecessary instability in our nation. Instead, the Chief of Chiefs has agreed that come the next *Serikali*,

	three cabinet posts will be reserved for religious organisations as follows: One for Muslims, one specifically for your Church and one for Counsellor Mama Mgei. What do you say to that?
Ben'sa:	I have nothing to say. Is it not *Serikali* that has been telling us to stick to the business of our calling?
Yuda:	Yes, Bishop, but you know these things are not cast in stone.
Ben'sa:	Precisely, it pleases me a great deal to know that *Serikali* is not asleep, that it is very much aware of what is happening in our country. I am also happy that for once the Church is being recognised as a place where national healing and reconciliation can take place. Only remember that in the matter of the hard politics of government to be or not to be becomes a matter of individual conscience.
Yuda:	That is partly why we are seeking your advice. Things are changing. The need for dialogue is beginning to be appreciated.
Ben'sa:	That is as it should be, but first we must stop this night running business and face reality. Night running activities do not qualify to be called dialogue. So my advice is this, lasting peace cannot be achieved through political intrigue, neither can it be achieved through harassment and

	intimidation. So just do unto others as you would have them do unto you. When one dialogue session fails, what guarantees the success of the next dialogue?
Mwodi:	But Bishop, out there is different. There you must form alliances with others for success. And to form alliances there must be dialogue. That is why dialogue has become a popular word in Kafira. And remember, once you form an alliance you cease to be yourself because you belong to the alliance even though the alliance doesn't necessarily belong to you.
Ben'sa:	I have said it and I will say it one more time: the business of the hard politics of government should be a matter of individual conscience. When I look at you two honourable gentlemen, I do not see politicians, no. Before me are two individuals who appear to have the same basic problem. Gentlemen, as politicians your problem is that you do not believe in what you are doing. I mean what do your alliances believe in, detention without trial?
Mwodi:	Well, those who consistently hit their heads against walls deserve to be put under protective detention.
Ben'sa:	Which walls has Pastor Mgei been hitting his head against?

Yuda:	Incitement is a very serious crime if you don't know. What was he inciting them to do? Well, this I cannot hide from you, *Serikali* was planning to set the pastor free until two weeks ago when he master-minded that mutiny at Manyinya prison.
Ben'sa:	Who? Pastor Mgei? How can anyone mastermind a mutiny two hundred miles away from where he is being detained?
Yuda:	Investigations are still going on. If he is found innocent, appropriate action will be taken.
Ben'sa:	Let me repeat for the third time, what I said a little while ago. Believe in yourselves and do unto others as you would have them do unto you.
Yuda:	Bishop, what we are saying is that...
Ben'sa:	Do unto others as you would have them do unto you, that should be the alpha and omega of human existence. Gentlemen that is all. *(Ben'sa rings a table bell and soon Sister Leah enters.)*
Yuda:	Bishop, we thank you, but may we request to come again?
Ben'sa:	You are good people, so if it becomes necessary that you come again, the door will be open. That is what I wish others to do unto me, leave the door open.
Mwodi & Yuda:	Thank you.

Ben'sa:	Thank you too. Sister Leah, please show the visitors to their cars. Gentlemen, my final advice is that you truthfully talk to Counsellor Mama Mgei as an individual who deserves respect. You will discover in time that truth can do wonders.
Yuda:	Thank you Bishop, you can be sure that that shall be done. *(Sister Leah leads the visitors out and soon returns.)*
Ben'sa:	I think we should arrange to devote next Sunday's prayers to *Serikali*.
Sister Leah:	Why?
Ben'sa:	They have lost belief in themselves. That seems to be the problem.
Sister Leah:	But why did you advise them to go and talk to Mama Mgei?
Ben'sa:	Promotion of the culture of dialogue. I think they are aware that the people have reached the point of no return.
Sister Leah:	So what are they intending to do?
Ben'sa:	That is the problem; they don't seem to know what to do. Last week's opinion polls must have rocked them to the marrow of their bones. Can you imagine that they now want to offer three cabinet posts to religious organisations?
Sister Leah:	It was wise of you to suggest recording, just in case.
Ben'sa:	I am sure they recorded it too.

Sister Leah:	Three cabinet positions! But how sure are they that the National Party will win the coming elections?
Ben'sa:	It is panic; they are beginning to panic because of last week's opinion polls. We should tell Mama Mgei to be careful.
Sister Leah:	But Mama Mgei is not the one conducting the opinion polls.
Ben'sa:	Sister, history has always been a good teacher. From our not too distant history, it is when *Serikali* is as nervous as it is now that prominent people begin to disappear or die in mysterious circumstances. At the moment, Mama Mgei is vulnerable.
Sister Leah:	But does she really intend to stand?
Ben'sa:	If she is cleared by our mother organisation and her conscience is clear, why should she not stand? After all the opinion polls are only indicating that the National party will lose, but they are not telling us who will win.
Sister Leah:	But the *Peoples Vision* newspaper stated that if any adult from the Mgei family stood on any ticket except the National Party ticket, that person would win.
Ben'sa:	Sister, what we need is peace, and then we can all be winners. With prayers, all things are possible. Let us pray. *(They kneel down as curtains close.)*

SCENE THREE

Revelations

This is another roadside scene on the same road as in scene one. This time the two cars are arriving from the opposite direction from where they were headed in scene one. This time it is Mwodi's car that arrives first. He gets out as soon as he stops the car. Yuda arrives soon after and they immediately engage in a conversation.

Yuda: Hon. Mwodi, I think we need to be more organised when we work together on a sensitive issue like this one.

Mwodi: So what is it this time? The blame game again?

Yuda: It is not the blame game again. I don't know how or when that expression stole its way into our national bank of expressions. I mean, I clearly told you that Bishop Ben'sa was a highly intelligent woman. Now, when I said that I had not missed going to church since the beginning of the year, you didn't have to say what you said.

Mwodi: What did I say?

Yuda: You said you attended church religiously.

Mwodi: Aah, religiously? Did I say religiously?

Yuda:	Yes, religiously until you got involved in that accident. Do you know that that is what made the bishop begin to doubt our credibility? That is what made her bring up that subject of waking up and doing or not doing things. So you tell me, what do you do when you wake up early?
Mwodi:	Honourable Yuda, waking up is waking up. Do I need to do anything to show that I have woken up?
Yuda:	No, you don't need to. That is why I am uncomfortable about this whole business. That meeting with Bishop Ben'sa is already bothering me. It has made me begin to doubt myself. Why I am alive, what I believe in and where I am going. Hon. Mwodi, what do you as an individual believe in?
Mwodi:	Eh, my brother, don't do that. It is that kind of question that causes people heart attacks. Is it your desire that I die now?
Yuda:	God forbid, no. Why would I desire your death?
Mwodi:	That is what I want to know.
Yuda:	I would not desire your death because at least you are redeemable.
Mwodi:	Redeemable?
Yuda:	Yes, you and I are redeemable for as long as we take the courage to think independently.

Mwodi:	I don't understand you.
Yuda:	Do you want to understand me?
Mwodi:	Yes.
Yuda:	Okay. (*He fiddles with his belt as if to switch off something.*) Now this is off the records, strictly between you and me, okay?
Mwodi:	Okay.
Yuda:	Let us start with alliances. If alliances deny you your individuality what are you left with?
Mwodi:	Stress. If they deny you your individuality, you will definitely be left with stress.
Yuda:	That is true. So between you and me, alliances are rich grounds for the transfer and spread of stress from one set of individuals to another. Once we have established that, what do you think should be the way forward?
Mwodi:	Well, since there are no walls with ears here, it is my turn to call a spade a spade. Bishop Ben'sa told us that truth is heavenly but, of course, we are deaf. She was right, you know, truth is heavenly, but we should remember that it takes long for us to recognise and accept it.
Yuda:	That in fact is truth itself. You know talking to that woman this evening has softened something inside me.

Mwodi:	Me too, most of what she said makes sense, but only outside of politics. It reminds me of that business of eating your cake and having it still. *(Pause)* You know what I would do if I could?
Yuda:	What?
Mwodi:	Resign.
Yuda:	Resign now? No brother, resignation is out of question, no one abandons an alliance just like that. What reasons would you give and who would listen to you?
Mwodi:	Look at it this way: the ballot is around the corner and the voter has taken the centre stage. No one with political ambitions would want to antagonise the Kafiran voter at the moment.
Yuda:	What do you mean?
Mwodi:	I think that woman is not only a mind reader but a witch as well.
Yuda:	I think I agree with you this time, I mean we spent less than thirty minutes with her and yet your mind is already bubbling with strange ideas.
Mwodi:	It is the desire to believe in something, in myself.
Yuda:	That may be the case, but you must first defend your seat. We have just completed the first leg of our mission. Who knows how many more legs are left of the mission?

Mwodi:	It is a question of reading the signs of the times and making a final decision. But all said and done, I wish the Chief of Chiefs had chosen someone else instead of me.
Yuda:	It is called trust. You and I are trusted servants of the state.
Mwodi:	Patriots you mean?
Yuda:	What has patriotism got to do with trust?
Mwodi:	Remember the Koru operation? You were honoured with a state commendation weren't you? You were given a medal. What about me? Wasn't I there too? Who came up with the master plan that led to the apprehension of those tribal warmongers? My brother, unless you bought that medal, it means you were more trusted, more of a patriot than me.
Yuda:	I am sorry Hon. Mwodi, I was equally shocked to see names of people who had nothing to do with that operation being honoured. I didn't realise your name was missing until it was too late.
Mwodi:	But you were one of the few who saw the list before it was sealed and made official.
Yuda:	That is what I have just told you. I did not see the list until it was too late. Anyway, you should not allow such bitter thoughts to crowd your mind at a time like this. It is the kind of thought that makes one to lose belief in oneself. Come let's go,

I'm sure the Chief of Chiefs is anxiously waiting for us. *(Yuda pats Mwodi on the shoulder and they walk to their respective vehicles and drive off.)*

ACT TWO: SCENE ONE

Testimonies

(Dawn is breaking at The Green Cross Clinic. In the background are makeshift canvas structures such as the ones commonly used by internally displaced people. A few Rejects are kneeling down with their hands raised high above their heads in silent prayer. Their leader, Mama Mgei, presides over the meeting. She holds a sheet of paper which she refers to from time to time. Silence prevails. Suddenly she speaks and the Rejects repeat her words. From one of the wings, Mwodi and Yuda can be seen eavesdropping.)

Mama Mgei:	Creed of The Green Cross
Rejects:	Creed of The Green Cross.
Mama Mgei:	Being a child of the universe.
Rejects:	Being a child of the universe.
Mama Mgei:	I believe in Nature and in the ideals of The Green Cross.
Rejects:	I believe in Nature and the ideals of The Green Cross.
Mama Mgei:	Conserving, nurturing and protecting the greenness of the earth.
Rejects:	Conserving, nurturing and protecting the greenness of the earth.

Mama Mgei:	Nurturing and protecting honesty, truth and justice with all my sensibilities.
Rejects:	Nurturing and protecting honesty, truth and justice with all my sensibilities.
Mama Mgei:	Believing that if all humankind toil and suffer together, the individual does not suffer.
Rejects:	Believing that if all humankind toil and suffer together, the individual does not suffer.
Mama Mgei:	May it be so now and forever.
Rejects:	May it be so now and forever.
Mama Mgei:	Truth, our everlasting green guide.
Rejects:	Truth, our everlasting green guide.
Mama Mgei:	Amen.
Rejects:	Amen.
Mama Mgei:	Thank you. You will remember that last evening I deliberately chose not to answer the question asked by Reject number five. The answer is yes, but you must also remember that we still live in Kafira where everything is secret until it becomes public. *(To Reject Five)* Are you satisfied with that answer?
Reject Five:	Yes, I am.
Mama Mgei:	Good. Now the theme of our meditation this morning is forgiveness. As you meditate, remember that not only those who forgive deserve to be forgiven. As

human beings, created in our Creator's image, we all deserve to be forgiven. So here is your individual assignment: think of at least two changes that you currently desire to see in Kafira today. For every change, identify individuals or institutions that appear to be against that particular change. Finally, pray genuinely for the identified individuals and institutions, for you strongly believe that they know not what they are doing. When you think you are through, go into the usual groups and compare your views. Do you have any questions?

Rejects: No.

Mama Mgei: Alright, it is meditation time. *(The Rejects leave and go to sit in a semi-circle in a prepared space on the stage, each engrossed in deep thought. Mwodi and Yuda approach Mama Mgei.)*

Mama Mgei: I feel the cold blood of strangers in my presence. Come, you are welcome to the clinic of The Green Cross.

Yuda: May the day break, Counsellor Mama Mgei.

Mama Mgei: May it break indeed. You are welcome.

Yuda & Mwodi: Thank you.

Mama Mgei: I wonder what brings you to this humble home of lunatics so early in the morning.

Mwodi: Lunatics?

Mama Mgei:	Yes, lunatics. Is that not what you people in *Serikali* prefer to call me and my patients? For you in *Serikali* it seems everyone with contrary views to yours is a lunatic.
Mwodi:	I think you are mistaken, Mama Mgei. We in *Serikali* have the greatest respect for what you do here. The only problem is when you unnecessarily engage in hard politics.
Mama Mgei:	Hard politics?
Yuda:	Yes, and since you can't stay clear of the hard politics of our time, we have good news for you.
Mama Mgei:	Good news? Is my husband now a free man then?
Yuda:	Patience, Mama Mgei, patience. *(Pause)* We do not wish to waste your time, so I will call a spade a spade. You see, after long hours of deliberations, *Serikali* has finally decided to legalise your participation in hard politics. The Chief of Chiefs has decided to extend an olive branch to you.
Mama Mgei:	Olive branch! That sounds nice.
Yuda:	We have decided to offer you a full cabinet post in the next *Serikali*. In fact, we will reserve three cabinet posts for religious organisations as follows: one for you, one for Muslims and the other for Christians. So Mama, take some time and think seriously about the offer. *(Pause)* Is it a deal or no deal?

Mama Mgei:	No deal. You people in *Serikali* are living in a totally different world from the one we live in. When were elections held? Who told you that you or the Chief of Chiefs will decide who will be in the next *Serikali*?
Mwodi:	That is why we are here. We came to consult you and to strike a deal on the way forward.
Mama Mgei:	You came to consult me as who?
Mwodi:	Mama Mgei, everyone knows you are one of the opinion leaders in Kafira.
Mama Mgei:	Too little too late.
Mwodi:	Too little too late? Is that what you think?
Mama Mgei:	Yes. Only a fool runs after a train that has already departed.
Mwodi:	But why, I mean, how...?
Mama Mgei:	*(Pointing to where the Rejects are seated.)* Answers to those questions are over there. Come and I will show you what you have refused to see over the years. Come and I will introduce you to the realities of Kafira, our motherland. *(She leads the two to where the Rejects are seated. One by one she invites the Rejects to narrate the story of their misery.)*
Mama Mgei:	This is Reject number one, perceived dissident by you in *Serikali*. Number one, you have a voice, speak. *(A young, clean-shaven man timidly stands and speaks.)*

Reject One: I was trained as a policeman. At the station where I was posted, all my colleagues were also my friends. That is what I believed. Soon, it dawned on me that most of my colleagues were averse to truth and honesty. I became lonely and disillusioned since I could not stand their stories of daily adventure. One afternoon, as I returned from duty, I saw one of the houses at the station on fire. The fire had just started. As I ran towards the burning house, women were screaming all around me, saying that there was a child inside the house. I snatched a bucket of water from someone, poured the water on myself and dashed inside. By good luck, the little girl was standing in the corridor, scared to death. I rescued the child and was pleasantly surprised when three days later I was promoted and awarded a medal. Later that week, stories began circulating at the station that I was a shrewd thief. The father of the child I had rescued claimed that he had left two thousand shillings in a drawer in the house, but soon after the rescue mission the money was missing. Although I denied opening any drawers in the smouldering house, my colleagues at the station chose not to believe me. One evening as I walked back to the station I was ambushed by hooded people and beaten up. When I got back to my house, I armed myself and went in search of my assailants. It was then that I was disarmed and summarily dismissed from the force. My uncle knew of this place. He is the one who recommended that I come here for a short while.

Mama Mgei: There is a typical lunatic for you. *(Moves to the next Reject.)* Reject Four, you have a voice, speak.

Reject Four: I am a born again lover of nature. I am told that ever since I was a toddler, I had a natural fascination for natural things: the slow but sure upward growth of frail seedlings; the communal humming of bees as they sadly fly away from one home to the next, evicted by sleepless charcoal burners; the happy singing of greetings by birds from different trees at dawn; the poetic beginnings of a tropical storm, even the thunder that tore the sky before my very eyes; that for me was second heaven. I grew up and joined the Green Movement. Our leader then was a humble and selfless old woman. One day the old woman led us in planting seedlings where *Serikali* had cut hundreds of trees to export to our neighbours up north. It was a fine sunny morning, so we sang happily as we planted the seedlings. Suddenly, very suddenly, an irate group of men and women descended on us with crude weapons. They beat us up and left us for dead. We needed gradual natural healing and so some of us chose to come here. Fortunately that planting was not in vain because one day our leader was well rewarded by those whom God has endowed with natural wisdom and knowledge. That day every Kafiran cried tears of joy and of pride.

Mama Mgei: *(To the two officials.)* That was not too long ago. You should remember it vividly since it was widely covered by the local and international media. That is how we in Kafira manufacture our national lunatics. *(Mwodi appears to wipe tears from his eyes.)*

Mwodi: I think I am losing it.

Yuda: What?

Mwodi: Excuse me.

Mama Mgei: Reject number five, talk to us.

Reject Five: I have nothing to say about what they said I had done. How could I incite my own students to riot? That is what I was accused of. *(Pointing to Reject Three)* He is better placed to speak on the matter since he was the first prosecution witness. But I have forgiven him. I have forgiven the others as well, I have forgiven them all.

Mama Mgei:	*(Pointing at Reject Three who appears to be absent-minded.)* Number three here has not uttered a word since we admitted him... He was a brilliant student leader. He is said to have been one of those who implicated number five in the riots. He is yet to recover fully from his experience after the Rector was found guilty and dismissed from his job.
Reject Three:	*(Standing up and trembling with rage.)* I want to talk, I must speak. *(He addresses Reject Five.)* My Rector, did I hear you say you had forgiven me? Thank you, thank you, and thank you again. Now I will be able to sleep. But, please, whatever you do, don't forgive the others because they don't deserve to be forgiven. They would betray you again if they had the chance, please don't forgive them. They came to my room at night and said they wanted to change my life once and for all, and having lived in poverty all my life I got tempted. I accepted the money and agreed to be coached. When we missed classes for two weeks I was told it was because you were supporting the lecturers' strike. That is when they asked me to lead a students' demonstration with your permission.
Reject Five:	That demonstration was supposed to be peaceful; it was not supposed to be violent.

Reject Three:	Ooh, son of a peasant, I am done. I am finished. I am Judas Iscariot.
Reject Five:	*(Patting Reject Three on the shoulder.)* Young man, you pull yourself together. You are a brave young man who has discovered his voice. Pull yourself together. For as long as you are still under the care of this mother of mothers, the future is still virgin for you. *(To Mama Mgei)* Mother of mothers, we will never thank you enough for babysitting Kafira's rejects.
Mama Mgei:	Number two, it is your turn.
Reject Two:	I was a trade unionist, fighting for the welfare of the goose that lays the eggs. They called me a stumbling block because I refused to sign a tendering lie for the construction of an administration block at our headquarters. It did not take long before I was dismissed from my position and charged with fraud.
Mama Mgei:	The story of my husband's detention is not different. It is common knowledge that before the Missionaries of The Green Cross returned to their country, they decided to thank my husband for the work he had done for them. They donated this piece of land to him and asked him to continue offering selfless service to the deprived. After several years of deep reflection, Pastor Mgei decided to turn this place into a natural healing clinic for

38

troubled minds. That was his offence, being kind to perceived enemies of *Serikali*. For that reason *Serikali* suddenly became interested in this piece of land and when he held a demonstration against the impending high-handedness, you called it incitement and detained him.

Yuda: *Serikali* had noble intentions. We simply wanted to make the facility available for use by more Kafirans. We wanted to create the best modern City Park in the region, but your husband chose to incite peace-loving Christians to violence.

Mama Mgei: It was a peaceful demonstration until your people came.

Yuda: The so called Christians threw stones at the security forces and burned innocent citizens' vehicles.

Mama Mgei: It is your word against mine. *(Pointing at the Rejects)* Look at them, these social rejects form only a small sample of who we have here. The majority of our patients are veteran lunatics and they reside in those tents over there.

Mwodi: Mama Mgei, excuse me, can we talk to you in private?

Mama Mgei: And why not? Come this way. *(She leads them off stage.)*

***

(Enter Sikia Macho the narrator)

Sikia Macho: The consultations that were held between the two officials from *Serikali* and Counsellor Mama Mgei were not the usual arm twisting games that Kafirans had for long been used to. Exactly two weeks following those consultations something totally unexpected happened in Kafira. The media carried various stories about the registration of a new political party called the Gender Party of Kafira (GPK). Following that revelation, there were spontaneous street celebrations throughout Kafira. The following day, the Registrar of Political Parties, Madam Arasa J. Arasa was summoned and summarily dismissed from her job. She was clearly going bananas and needed state protection. It was then that all hell seemed to break loose. A few *Serikali* officials gathered courage and resigned from their jobs, the most prominent one of them being honourable Mwodi arap Mwodi. Yes, Mwodi had finally abandoned the alliance to which he had sworn to be a life member. By this time the only ember left in the fireplace of the ruling regime was to eat humble pie and release both Madam Arasa J. Arasa and Pastor Mgei. This became the daily clarion call of most Kafirans. It was loud and it was clear.

***

SCENE TWO

Dream of Reality

This is a typical room at a detention camp. Two inmates, Mgei and Adema sit facing different directions, each in deep thought. Suddenly, Adema appears to break down crying.

Adema: I have reached it, yes, I have reached it.

Mgei: Hmm, what?

Adema: I have reached the point of no return! *(Mgei goes and pulls him up.)*

Mgei: Hey, man, what is the matter? What are you talking about? What is the problem?

Adema: I have made up my mind and there is no going back.

Mgei: You have made up your mind?

Adema: Yes.

Mgei: To do what?

Adema: Confess. I want to confess and be done with it.

Mgei: Okay, please calm down. Just calm down and tell me what you want to confess. *(Pause)* What is it you want to confess?

Adema: Anything. All they want is for us to confess before they set us free. So let them have their cake and eat it. Let them tell me what to confess and I will do so without delay. That soldier said if we confess they will hire someone to help us to confess with dignity.

Mgei: Confession with dignity? George, my schoolmate, look at me, do you know who I am?

Adema: You are an innocent criminal, but that doesn't help does it?

Mgei: Our covenant, have you forgotten our covenant?

Adema: But it is not just about you and me, it's the whole village, you know. They were even planning to slaughter two bulls to welcome me and the degree. My schoolmate, it is my children's pride that I am thinking about now. They have invested so much in my adult education that I can't afford to let them down. I was going to be the first from the village to get that piece of paper, you know. God, what a disappointment! Pastor, my schoolmate, can't you see that I have let an entire village down?

Mgei: George, what we are doing is more important than the aspirations of a clan, or a village. What we did and are still doing is for our motherland, for all Kafirans. It is more important than a piece of paper because sacrifice is a score in the mind.

It should be an eternal source of pride, so take some time to think seriously about it. Persevere for a week or so, just persevere.

Adema: But why, what for?

Mgei: Because confessing to something you have not done is a form of personal betrayal, a bribe, and I don't think you are that kind of person. My schoolmate, you are not that kind of person. You joined us because you believed in our course; it was a question of human rights. You saw the injustice and you chose to join us, so what is it you want to confess?

Adema: After graduation I can always come back.

Mgei: That means you haven't learnt much from our recent history. My schoolmate, listen, I have fresh intelligence from the Good One. (Showing him a small stone on which there is a coded message.) Look, the new party is agitating for our release.

Adema: Agitating, that could be reason enough for our total elimination. Didn't the Good One also say Mwodi had been arrested?

Mgei: That may be so, but it also means they are running out of options. (Yawns loudly.) God, I am tired, I need some rest. So do you, my schoolmate. (Pause) Whose turn is it to pray to night?

Adema: Mine. But I have nothing more to ask for.

Mgei:	Persistence, we must persist. Remember: He helps only those who help themselves.
Adema:	Alright, let us bow our heads and pray. *(They close their eyes and bow their heads.)* Lord, our God, only you know and understand the dynamics of our current situation. Let thy will be done. I ask this through the name of your son, Jesus Christ.
Both:	Amen. *(They move to their respective places of rest, say goodnight to each other and lie down to sleep. After some time, Mgei appears to have a nightmare. He jumps up violently and stares blankly at something by the door. The figure of Mwodi with a Bible raised high above his head can be seen in the doorway.)*
Mwodi:	*(Repeatedly as he moves towards Mgei.)* So help me God, so help me God, so help me God... *(Sees Mgei and is immediately humbled. He puts the Bible under his left armpit and salutes with the right hand.)* Your Excellency, I am sorry I am late, but that is because we had to take care of your safety first. It was quite tricky. To secure your release we needed to sacrifice and replace you with someone else. Yes, we needed a scapegoat and we being rather thin on the ground, I volunteered to be that scapegoat. We begged Yuda to go

and report that I was leaking important information to Bishop Ben'sa and to your wife, Counsellor Mama Mgei. That worked wonders. Without bothering to investigate the matter, I was immediately arrested and sent to various places before they finally decided to bring me here. That was two days ago. It was a watertight plan and I believe it still is a watertight plan. I would not be surprised if Hon. Yuda is now a very powerful man in *Serikali. (Whispering)* I am in cubicle number 22, next to the chapel. Good luck Your Excellency, please don't forget me. *(He turns and quickly exits.)*

Mgei: *(Running after him)* Wait, hey you, wait! *(Confused he stands still rubbing his eyes. Slowly, he resumes his sleeping position. After some time, he wakes up normally and tiptoes to where his colleague is asleep.)* Schoolmate, comrade, wake up, wake up.

Adema: What, what is it?

Mgei: A nightmare, I have just had a terrible dream.

Adema: Are you waking me up because of a dream?

Mgei: Well, you know they say reality is sometimes stranger than fiction. I don't know

	whether it was a dream or a figment of my imagination.
Adema:	What is the difference? Do you know that is treasonable?
Mgei:	*(Laughing)* Yes, I remember there was a time when the imagination of certain things was treasonable in Kafira. Yes, that imagination of mine, that one of "so help me God" with Hon. Mwodi would have sent me straight into detention.
Adema:	Whose death did you imagine?
Mgei:	There was no death, only imagination. The question of human rights gave birth to the fear. You know it was very sad. Very sad because the fear that grew in the minds of the children of that time is the fear that sits in the minds of the adults of today.
Adema:	What are you talking about?
Mgei:	I am talking about professional cowardice. That is the worst thing that can ever happen to a nation's professionals.
Adema:	You know you are absolutely right. I once had an opportunity to sit on a committee that was vetting books for a literary prize. One of the books was rejected because the author was a well-known anti-government columnist in a local weekly newspaper. *(Laughs)* Do you know why the second book was rejected?

Mgei:	No, most likely no money had been poured.
Adema:	No, you are wrong. The second book was rejected because of professional cowardice. One of the sub-themes of the book was political succession. To some of the panellists that was a taboo subject since the general elections were just around the corner.
Mgei:	But you should have stuck to your guns.
Adema:	I did, but most of them claimed that they were saving the author from detention.
Mgei:	What hypocrisy! And so you just gave up?
Adema:	Someone suggested that since Kafira was a democratic country, we needed to vote on the matter. We voted and it ended there.
Mgei:	If there must be detention that was a clear case for detention. Members of that committee deserved to be detained for denying the author their prize.
Adema:	That is correct, because when the individual fear of a few cowards becomes institutionalised, it leads to the irreversible ignorance of an entire generation.
Mgei:	My suspicion is that the panellists had not even read the books.
Adema:	That is a very real possibility, in which case they deserved double detention.

You too deserve to be detained twice for waking me up because of a dream. You know when a disturbed mind finally submits to sleep, it is time for busybodies to show respect and retreat.

Mgei: I am sorry; I shouldn't have woken you up. That was very insensitive of me.

Adema: What sort of dream was it anyway?

Mgei: I talked to Hon. Mwodi. Well, he talked to me. Maybe I am going bananas. Let's talk about it during break tomorrow morning.

Adema: Alright.

Mgei: Whose turn is it to pray tonight?

Adema: We have already prayed.

Mgei: I am sorry, goodnight.

Adema: Goodnight. *(They go to their respective sleeping places.)*

***

(Enter Sikia Macho)

Sikia Macho: As I have said before, no one knows what Hon. Mwodi and Hon. Yuda discussed with Counsellor Mama Mgei. But it would appear that the two officials are no ordinary mortals, they were double edged swords. Somehow the two seem to have agreed that in order to cleanse themselves, one would have to betray the other while the other would feign shock and disappointment. As Adema had prayed the night he wanted to confess, the Lord seemed to have let His will be done. Pastor Mgei was released from detention with a stern warning not to participate in any political activities. But that was too little too late. By this time Kafirans had seen the light. They were not about to be returned to the dark days of lack of belief in themselves. Pastor Mgei was soon declared the sole Presidential candidate of the newly formed GPK which had now officially changed its name to the Green Party of Kafira. In a game of political intrigue they say only those that bite off what they can chew survive. The rest perish in the scramble for visibility. *(A cocktail of musical instruments can be heard from afar.)* Listen, can you hear them? Those are the jubilant supporters of the Green Party of Kafira. They seem confident that no one will deny them victory come voting day tomorrow. Aeh, wait a minute. *(He fumbles in his flat chest bag and finally retrieves his ID and Voter's Cards.)* For a moment I thought a common thief had disabled me, but here they are: my ID and my voter's cards. I am sure you know who to vote for. As

for me, I will go to bed early to avoid
the inconvenience of a long queue. But
remember if it happens, if it does not
happen, we still have our lives to live. *(He
exits).*

SCENE THREE

The Unexpected Reward

The Rejects are rehearsing a dance for performance at the swearing in ceremony of Pastor Mgei the President-elect. The dance choreographer enters and gives a few instructions to the dancers.

Choreographer: Are you ready for the final rehearsal?

Rejects: *(Enthusiastically)* Yes, we are.

Choreographer: Good, Mama will soon be here to watch us. *(Noticeable excitement among the dancers.)* Remember this dance is in honour of all those Kafiran heroes who will not be with us tomorrow because they chose to shake hands with truth. So let your bodies describe the joy of victory even in death. Yes, this is a symbolic dance that should speak directly to the sensibilities of all. Mama will be here shortly to grace our final rehearsal. You may now go and prepare. You will enter when I blow the whistle. *(The Rejects leave. The Choreographer fetches two chairs and puts them in place. Mama Mgei enters and is shown to her chair. The Choreographer takes her own chair and blows the whistle. The Rejects perform a stunning dance*

51

	that lasts about three to four minutes, depending on how captivating it is. At the end of the dance, Mama and the Choreographer give the troop a standing ovation.)
Mama Mgei:	Very well done. At last the stone that was scoffed at and ignored shall become the cornerstone. Let me assure you now that I have the official invitation, from now you are official guests of the state. You will need to prepare quickly because your transport will be here within an hour. You will be brought back here the day after the swearing-in ceremony. That is when you will be told how each one of you will be compensated for your honesty and courage. Thank you and good luck. *(Wild cheers from the dancers)* But remember that humility is the salt that makes success a desired goal. *(Mama goes off, escorted by the Choreographer as the Rejects hug one another excitedly.)*
Choreographer:	*(After returning)* Our final rehearsals shall be...
Reject Five:	*(Humourously)* In detention! *(All laugh hilariously.)*
Choreographer:	Our final rehearsal shall be where we will be accommodated. *(Muted laughter,*

You may go and prepare for departure. *(Dancers leave)*

***

(Enter Sikia Macho)

Sikia Macho: What you have just seen is evidence of the resolve of Kafirans on that voting day. People refused to sleep because they wanted to stand up and be counted, and counted they were. It is even rumoured that expectant women gave birth as they waited to vote. It was a right that they desperately clung to. And when the results were finally announced, the opinion polls had won. The Green Party of Kafira had won with an overwhelming majority. The National Party, let us give credit where it is due, had accepted the people's verdict and conceded defeat, paving the way for the swearing-in of the new president. And long before that swearing-in ceremony, Kafirans were beside themselves with expectation. It was a time of rebirth, a time of reconciliation and a time of hope. No one knew whose hand they had shaken vigorously because such knowledge would be of no use; it was a thing of the past. To tell you the truth, I can't wait for tomorrow. *(He exits.)*

SCENE FOUR

The Past Meets the Present

(This is the swearing-in ceremony. Several traditional troops can be heard approaching from different directions. The atmosphere is electric as the venue for the swearing-in ceremony is prepared. A bugle sounds and silence rules. Two children, a girl and a boy, in school uniform lead Pastor Mgei, president-elect, in. One of the children carries a Bible while the other one carries a shield. Mama Mgei follows Pastor Mgei closely. Yuda and Mwod follow the children closely. Bishop Ben'sa and the Rejects follow as the rest of the invited guests take their positions. As soon as Pastor Mgei is at the designated swearing-in spot, the child with the Bible hands it to Pastor Mgei. Pastor holds the Bible in his right hand and speaks.)

Mgei: So help me God. *(Bishop Ben'sa takes the Bible from Mgei and hands him another Bible. Raising the second Bible Mgei says,* So help me God. *Tremendous and sustained applause for the President elect. Mgei steps forward to address the nation.)* My fellow countrymen, after consultations with our advisers and our intended partners in development, we have decided that this swearing-in ceremony should be different from what Kafirans are used to. Because the word protocol has no equivalent in each of our ten national languages, we shall ignore it henceforth. But since you do not ignore something that you are used to without replacing it with something else, we have decided to replace the term protocol with the term common sense. That is why today, our advisers have seen it prudent that I be officially sworn in by Justice Arasa J. Arasa. (*Arasa steps forward and swears in the President. Tremendous applause follows the swearing in.*)

Mgei: My countrymen, the first duty of any well-meaning national leader is to restore the people's confidence in the rule of law. And since justice delayed is justice denied, I wish to boldly reinstate Prof. Tirus Bundotich as the Vice-Chancellor of Kafira State University of Natural Wisdom with immediate effect. Mr. Rector, that passionate request of yours is hereby granted.

Reject Five: (*Who is already adorned in an academic gown, holds a green academic cap in his hand. He signals to Adema who adorns a green academic gown to step*

	forward) From Kafira State University of Natural Wisdom, it is my pleasure to invite Your Excellency to confer on George Albert Adema, the degree of Master of Humility and Selflessness. *(He gives the cap to Pastor Mgei who confers the degree.)*
Mgei:	George Albert Adema I give you the power to read and do all that appertains to this degree. *(Wild ululations and cheers are heard as he confers the degree. Sikia Macho enters.)*
Sikia Macho:	It is always sad when a good thing comes to an end. But the end of a thing like what we have just witnessed is always a reminder of where we have come from, where we are, and where we are going. It is indeed from such reflections that we derive the energy to live on and on. Yes, it is joyous sadness, so help us God.

The End